LIBERTARIANISM

By

Susan P. Cummings

Look to nature for the answers!

https://twitter.com/Britanniacomms/status/720320188013522944

(Albert Einstein)

Table of Contents

Chapter 1
What is Libertarianism?

Voting in any election is very important, and equally important is to understand who you are voting for and what *they* stand for; and, you must first understand your position on the issues and the truth about those issues. Each political party, whether popular or not, visions for something in particular and in which they identify with. The Libertarian Party is closely complemented by Classic Liberalism and is beside the same ideas of what our Founding Fathers had believed; Individualism, Free Will, The Right to Property. Historically known as, *"Life, Liberty and Pursuit of Happiness."* These are just some of the ingredients that explain Libertarianism. In "O Libertarian, Where Is Thy Sting?" Author Jennifer Burns writes about the inception or creation of the Libertarian party, and the location of its beginning as being Denver, Colorado in 1971. She also mentions the various aspects or ideas that come from Libertarianism, and, their political involvement starting in the late 1960's and early 1970's. The author emphasizes the differences in *ideology* within the Libertarian party, and how each of these ideologies has its own thought. According to authors Nick Gillespie and Matt Welch in their article titled *"Tuned Out"* (pgs

26-30), because people are getting more and more frustrated with the *"status quo"* of both political parties, Democrat and Republican, more and more Americans are seeking alternatives and restoring the roots of America's founding. Gillespie and Welch also highlight that Americans are gravitating more toward self-reliance and independent living, *"The right to be left alone,"* which is the basis of Libertarian thought, and include the organization of government, education, social programs, and, laws and regulations are key components.

Chapter 2
The Different Ideologies

Lack of a strong stand on *Paternalism* is considered one of the weaknesses of the Libertarian Party, according to author Steven Wall in his article *"Self Ownership and Paternalism" (Pgs.399-417).* He discusses how Libertarianism is a belief that people own themselves; therefore, he or she is also responsible for oneself. If individuals want to do drugs then others should not intervene with this, mainly because it is that person's choice, whether it be self-destructive or not, and, any attempt to assist in any sort of rehabilitation is considered a violation of the persons' rights. This is one of a significant weakness of Libertarianism, especially in the eyes of those who are religious or have any kind of moral compass. It can be perceived as a cowardly or uncaring view toward humanity.

Within our society, we have a judicial system for those accused of doing wrong, and an equal means by way to defend oneself. Libertarians, according to author Erik Luna and Hugh B. Brown, *(Pgs.263-294),* do not believe in a *"Utilitarian deference,"* which is when the punishment is based upon the usefulness of a human being. Evan Riley wrote in her article titled "LibertarianSelf-Defeat *(Pgs.200-226),* that the Libertarian individual or Party should be committed to; *"The RSC (Reasonable Stability Criterion),"* which is, in a just society people will understand what is expected of them, and *"The MEC (Moral Education Condition),"* which is, the educational means for moral conditioning and is just another polite way of saying *Utilitarian deference*. It is very similar to *Paternalism* that author Steven Wall accuses the Libertarians of lacking. *Progressive* and *Fabian Socialists* believe that a person's worth is measured according to whether they are productive in society, as proclaimed by the late George Bernard Shaw (Prize.Org). *Socialism* is also another collective idea, but on the *"light"* side of Fabian Socialism. Libertarianism can be moderate to extreme, and other ideologies have their way of creeping in.

The Libertarian view between Laws and Morality can be clearly noted in an article titled *"Law and Moral Purpose"* by Robert P. George regarding social issues and where Libertarians stand on them. In particular, "the role of the government and non-government entities in family and community, abortion and marriage," and depending upon who you speak with and what end of the Libertarian spectrum you are on the answer to these social issues vary. This is one of the reasons Libertarians really do not have a clear-cut identity; but instead, have an identity problem. Author Peter Inwagen in an article he wrote, "How to Think About the Problem of Free Will", also defines this issue. It is important, once again, to note that the *"bad-terminology"* can be due to a mixture of ideas rather than the misuse of them, as described in his explanation. *"{Compatibilism and Incompatiblism},"* is *free-will affected by the events of the past or free-will as current thought?"* Peter Inwagen feels that the misinformation or characterization of Libertarians is due to *"bad terminology and confused ideas,"* which he states he has taken the term free-will *"from historically important positions."* Compatibilism being Gods sovereignty compatible to mans' freedom and relevant to pre-destination, and the opposite is Incompatiblism. *(Pgs.327-341).*

Libertarianism is not isolated to the so-called *"white America."* There is history of successful and powerful Black Americans who had the same ideology or vision as those of Libertarianism. For example, authors David T. Beito and Linda Royster-Beito *(Pgs.279-294)* wrote about the career of Rose Wilder Lane (1886-1968) at the Pittsburg Courier and how her ideas changed the thinking of the Republican Party. Rose Wilder Lane's disagreement in Franklin D. Roosevelt's (1882-1945) policies and her disconnect from the communist party. Lloyd Pratt also wrote a compelling story *(Pgs.47-52)* where he also writes a compassionate view of Frederick Douglass's (1818-1895) letters revealing Douglass's independent thoughts and ideas, also regarding Republicans, both of which are individualistic and had a significant impact on the changes within the Republican Party and the transition to Libertarianism; and Frederick Douglass's letter to his once enslaver historically pointing out Libertarian values and Individualisms.

One of the best examples that can be given of a true Libertarian is Senator Rand Paul of Kentucky. He ran under the Republican ticket because most of his views and stances are on the Right. Writer Jason Zengerie *(Pgs5-6)* depicts Senator Paul as a loony tune and not a *"traditional Libertarian."* He believes that the Senator has more radical views and stands for racial separation. Senator Rand Paul's father, Senator Ron Paul would better fit this description than his son, since Ron Paul has openly opposed the War on Drugs; would like to close all of our air and military bases around the world, and believes 9/11 was perpetrated by the U.S because of our involvement in Middle Eastern affairs. Rand Paul, who again as author Zengerie wrote about, is for legislatively outlawing abortion, while Ron Paul's views and ideas stand more on Isolationism. It is Rand Paul's father, Ron Paul who is the non-traditional Libertarian or as the author put it *"Paleo Wacko"* by our Founders standards. Senator Rand Paul actually represents the characteristics of Libertarianism more closely and accurately. While his father represents the Progressive aspect of

Libertarianism. Just like the Democrats have the Progressive Left (Socialism, Communism, Marxism), and the Republicans have their Progressive Right (Fascism, Nazism). The author may have either made a mistake in which of the Paul's he was describing, or the author's views are radical themselves.

In an article on *"the Phenomenon"* of the Tea Party, Benjamin Cunningham analyzes different factors of the Tea Party and the make-up of it. He claims the members are mostly Libertarian and anti-establishment; and he believes the members stem from the Republican Party. There have been news sources and outlets, and members of the Tea Party itself that have disputed this claim, and, have stated that the representation of the Tea Party is not anti-establishment, but rather, less government, and whose members belong to all political affiliations. In Cunningham's article he mentions the Tea Party to be all hard working Americans affected by the economy and the direction in which our country appears to be heading. The Tea Party Movement is not only about hard working people and the effects this economy has had on them, it is also about helping those who are less fortunate and who have been hit the hardest, i.e., the unemployed and the poor.

In other research of Libertarianism, and comparable to the aforementioned, it is found a certain form of Libertarianism to be destructive. It is in contrast to what Libertarianism is supposed to stand for. There are people with a certain mindset who delightfully infringe upon others and harass in the most intrusive ways. This form of Libertarianism is terroristic by definition and repulsive by nature. To benefit from another's loss, especially if you have participated in creating that loss, is considered unnatural. It creates an environment of chaos instead of harmony. It offends and endangers the innocent, such as children who have no choice but to be subjected to their parents' neglect and hostilities, rather than being taught respect and proper social behavior. This form of Libertarianism that is perceived as such is *Determinism*. It is used to alleviate an individual of all his or her responsibility of their actions, because it is understood to be pre-determined. This is not the case, of course. The Catholic Church believes in Determinism, but with individual responsibility as the Ten Commandments clearly state. (Theopedia: An Encyclopedia of Christianity) It is more of an excuse by those who may have had reigned over authority and now expect society to accept their *"bad behavior"* under the auspices of a *"right."*

Individuals of the Libertarian mindset, who are employed in positions of authority, often neglect and abuse that authority because their views have a much different twist than that of other citizens. Drug usage, prostitution, political agendas, and even terrorism is viewed as a personal choice; instead of potential threats to the general public. There is a clash between the mindsets in society. Sometimes this is done on purpose, or by design and the purpose can be cynical.

Chapter 3
Conclusion

Libertarianism is a political position for many, but for some it is a lifestyle. Some forms of libertarianism are in contrast to what our Founding Fathers had in mind when penning the Constitution and Declaration of Independence. Our founders were very clear about responsibility and respecting the rights of others. (*It is not the more radical forms of Libertarianism that make a person; it is the radical concept that may attract a certain type of person*). Libertarianism can be as close to Anarchism on one end of the spectrum, which was the original form of government in America, or to the extreme as Socialism or Marxism on the other end. Every political affiliation has its own variations from within. Libertarianism is no different and is experiencing birthing pangs. Because of the variations or different political ideologies, the idea of Liberty transforms itself; either individually or collectively.

Libertarianism is as old as the Roman Empire. As seen when Cicero addressed the Senate against Mark Antony by stating; *"How could a sane person first take up arms to destroy his country, and then protest because someone else had armed himself to save it?"* The concept of a Republic and Individualism and Natural Law, is the philosophy and Theology of many in that day. And, seen through the letter from one of Cicero's dearest friends and another Roman Statesman, Atticus, *"Friend to all, ally to none."*

Our Founding Fathers were extremely educated and read. And so many have been influenced in the making of a Republic and the Constitution by their fore-fathers. The concept of Libertarian thought and the understanding of Natural Law and Natures Law existed then, but what I believe is by Divine Providence has finally come to fruition because they understood history, our Founding Fathers, and the making of a Republic. It is bewildering to think that Libertarianism can be anything but what our Founders envisioned in our Constitution, and anything other than those visions is merely a hijacking for power and control. Individualism for mankind has been passed down from the Roman Philosophers to Jesus Christ (The Lord's Prayer) to our Founding Fathers. St. Francis, who is a "Mirror of Christ", speaks often of Individualism, and even though he decided to reject wealth, it wasn't wealth he was rejecting; it was himself. And the Pope of the Catholic Church today, Pope Francis, along with Pope Benedict XVl, depict the very essence of St. Francis's character and plight in restoring Christ's church.

One of the most outspoken and major architects of the American Revolution, Thomas Paine, was a true Libertarian and wrote many letters to Benjamin Franklin regarding the direction that America should take, and the rights to ownership (Lamb). In the author's article, Lamb describes Paine's beliefs to be both Libertarian and Socialist; however, the interpretation of Paine's theories or ideologies, as described by the author as *Egalitarian,* which by definition means equal rights in politics, social issues, economic, etc., and could have been confused with the *"equal right"* to pursue. Which is what I believe Paine was trying to get across in the new free world, rather than the *"equal right"* to possess, which is a socialist perspective. The *"right to pursue"* probably stems from his life in Britain and the freedoms not allowed by those of a different culture or class according to that society. The mere fact that Paine had come from Britain to America and then to incorporate the same political idea as that from which he came; and to initiate and participate in a revolution against the very government of which he fled, is revealing of the political ideology of Paine. The author's own socialistic views appear to be incorporated into a man's life unfairly. Thomas Paine famously wrote **"When the government fears the people it is Liberty, when the people fear the government it is Tyranny."** (American

Revival). If Paine really believed his own quote, then a need to fear tyranny or the government wouldn't have existed due to the ideology of egalitarianism. Paine's position can be better seen, according to Lamb, in one of Paine's most *"impressively argued works"* titled *Agrarian Justice.*

Like everything else in life, if pursued with care and conscience, true Libertarianism will once again have a place at the Constitutional table. To be a Libertarian is to understand what our Constitution really implies and teaches. It is about Individual freedoms, not the collective; it is about the right to pursue happiness without having to be privileged; It is about opportunity for all, but the outcomes are not guaranteed. That is up to the individual. It is about the rights that our Creator gave to us over the rights the government believes they have over us; it is understanding that when injustice have been done to anyone, by anyone, equal justice will be applied; It is not about everyone's pursuit, it is about one person to have the right to be responsible for themselves and their families, and to ensure prosperity (future generations). But, most of all, it is about respecting those who have sacrificed so much so we may always live free. This is what Libertarianism is; Respect, Responsibility and *"Securing the Liberty for ourselves and those of our Posterity."* (U.S. Constitution/Bill of Rights).

Chapter 4

Poem "In God We Trust"

(To all Americans)
A child kneels beside their bed
In prayer, bowing their head.
First Communion a child boasts
They received the Holy Ghost.
Confirmation is another step
In the plight, for our prep.
Choosing a favorite Saints name
Hopefully, it will not be in vain.
College brings many points of view
Choosing politics or God is all new.
I cannot ignore my heart or beliefs.
For he has always been my relief
People always try to eliminate his name
I believe it is for all that he came.
(God Bless America)

Susan P. Cummings

CITATIONS

American Revival. MMX. 20 Aug 2012. <www.americanrevival.org>.

Beito, David T., Beito, Linda Royster. "Selling Laissez-faire Antiracism to the Black Masses: Rose Wilder Lane and the Pittsburgh Courier." *Independent Review* 15.2 (2010): 279-294. Academic Search Premier. 17 August 2012.

Burns, Jennifer. "O Libertarian, Where Is Thy Sting?" *Journal Of Policy History* 19.4 (2007): 452 - 470. Academic Search Premier, 16 Aug 2012. 17 August 2012. <http://search.ebscohost.com.lib.kaplan.edu/login.aspx?direct=true&db=aph&AN=277686218&site=ehost.live>.

Cunningham, Benjamin. "More Magic than Movement." *New Presence: The Prague Journal of Central European Affairs* 12.2 (2010): 21-25. Academic Search Premier. 17 August 2012.

George, Robert P. "Law and Moral Purpose." *First Things: A Monthly Journal of Religion & Public Life* 179 (2008): 22-28. Academic Search Premier. 17 August 2012.

Gillespie, Nick, Welch, Matt. "Tuned Out (cover story)." *Politics (Campaigns & Elections);* 29.3 (2008): 26 - 30. Ronald Reagan, 1911-2004, Academic Search Premier. 17 August 2012.

Inwagen, Peter. "How To Think About The Problem of Free Will." *Journal of Ethics* 12.3/4 (2008): 327-341. Academic Search Premier. 17 August 2012.

Lamb, R. "Liberty, Equality, and the Boundaries of Ownership: Thomas Pain's Theory of Property Rights." *Review of Politics* 3.72 (2010): 483-511. Academic Research Premier. 20 August 2012.

Luna, Erik, Brown, Hugh B. "Traces Of a Libertarian Theory of Punishment." *Marquette Law Review* 91.1 (2007): 263 - 294. Academic Search Premier. 17 August 2012.

New World Encyclopedia. 6, 17 June, August 2008, 2012. 17 August 2012.

Pratt, Lloyd. "Human Beyond Understanding: Frederick Douglass's New Liberal Individual." *Novel: A Forum on Fiction* 43.1 (2010): 47-52. Academic Search Premier. 17 August 2012.

Prize.Org, Nobel. *George Bernard Shaw-Biography.* 2012. Nobel Lectures. 17 Aug 2012.

Riley, Evan. "Libertarian Self-Defeat." *Journal of Moral Philosophy* 7.2 (2010): 200-226. Academic Search Premier. 17 August 2012.

Theopedia: An Encyclopedia of Christianity. n.d. Licenced CC By 3.0. 17 August 2012.

Vallentyne, Peter. *Libertarianism*. Ed. Edward N. Zalta. Spring 2012. 17 August 2012.

Wall, Steven. "Self Ownership and Paternalism." *Journal of Poilitical Philosophy* 17.4 (2009): 399- -417. Academic Search Premier. 17 Aug 2012.

Zengerie, Jason. "Paleo Wacko." *New Republic* 241.10 (2010): 5-6. Academic Search Premier. 17 Aug 2012.

DEDICATION

Dedicated to all those who have fought tirelessly to protect our Freedoms, here and abroad...throughout history, for The Republic, for which we stand, of the United States of America.

GOD, COUNTRY and FAMILY...Amen